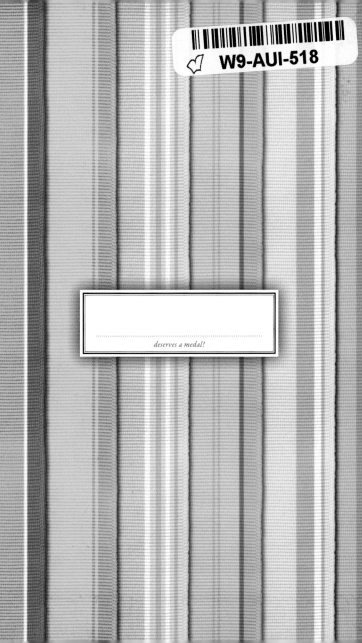

*deserves a medal!*

YOU DESERVE A MEDAL

Published by
Knock Knock
1635-B Electric Avenue
Venice, CA 90291
www.knockknockstuff.com

This book is based on actual experiences — many of them mine, but also those
of my brilliant friends, and my excellent editor and publisher, Jen Bilik.
Thank you from the bottom of my bruised and battered heart to Jed Alger,
Marian Bantjes, Lenny Feldsott, Karla Field, Lisa Jann, Andy Mallett,
David Mayes, Jennifer Morita, Steven Moss, Maggie Powers, Cathy Solarana,
Jennifer Stone, Terry Stone, Emily Wong, Suzanne Wertheim, and Doyald
Young. As always, *Vielen Dank* to my Mom *&* Dad, who have bravely endured
and foolishly encouraged my own Search for True Love from the very start.

Thank you also (and in some cases, again) to Suzanne Wertheim, Jed Alger,
Martha Rich, Jeff McMillan, and Emily Wong for giving generously of their
time and their genius as I wrestled with an early version of this book.

A deep bow of respect and gratitude to my wonderful and patient friends
at Knock Knock—Jen Bilik, Craig Hetzer, Megan Carey, Shane Beagin,
Brad Serum, and Elyse Tepper—for recognizing the pressing need for Medals
of Love and for investing so much tender, loving care into this project.

The Quest for Love is not for the faint of heart! It's a maddening
combination of playing the lottery, picking locks, and wrestling
the occasional dyspeptic gator. But then there are the good bits, too.
Good luck out there!

—*Stefan G. Bucher*

ISBN 978-160106126-3
UPC 825703-50003-5

10  9  8  7  6  5  4  3  2  1

# YOU DESERVE A MEDAL

## HONORS ON THE PATH TO TRUE LOVE

Written & Illustrated by
**STEFAN G. BUCHER**

**KNOCK KNOCK**®
knockknockstuff.com

## TABLE OF CONTENTS

# THE MEDALS

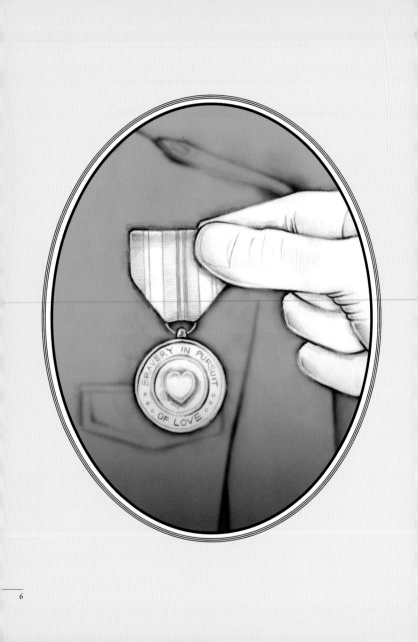

## YOU DESERVE AN INTRODUCTION

For over two thousand years, heroic deeds and extraordinary service have been rewarded with medals. What began as a way for military leaders to acknowledge their valiant troops was soon adopted to reward athletes victorious in competition. Much later, political, civic, and cultural achievements were added to the medal-worthy list. Medals have served to honor those who excelled, to inspire competitors and combatants to reach higher and work harder, to distinguish publicly those with honorable records behind them. Medals have found their paths to diverse spheres of influence, but the key word is "influence"—as a rule, to receive a medal, one has needed to impact many people, whether by leading them, besting them, saving them, killing them softly, or by just killing them outright.

But what of more personal victories and accomplishments? Do they not require equal bravery and stamina? Is not the quest for love, for example, every bit as fraught with peril and sublime in spirit as any martial or athletic undertaking? What army could match the destruction wreaked by a cold, hard stare from one's lover? What struggle is more savage than that against one's own romantic insecurities? What race presents more obstacles than that for the heart of another?

Fortunately, the turn of the twentieth century finally saw the introduction of awards and decorations to honor meritorious conduct and outstanding achievements in this, the search for true love. Established by Søren Linnæus and Edward George Goodwin in 1894 (see "You Deserve a Love Medal—Says Who?", pages 24–25), the Council of Romantic Decorations (CRD) has since been issuing medals to honor acts of personal heroism on the long and dangerous road to love.

To keep pace with the changing mores of our age, these medals have evolved and expanded over the years, building on the council's first honor, the Worst-of-Times Medal for Breakup Survival, to encompass modern-day battlefields of dating, telecommunications, premarital cohabitation, and that most fearsome invention of the atomic age, angst. At the same time, other medals have been retired due to progressive irrelevance. As methods of modern love have changed, so have the awards that commemorate them.

Despite their ubiquity, most of these decorations have until now remained out of the public eye. A few reasons can be hypothesized for such oversights: an antiromantic bias on the part of mainstream phaleristics scholars, obsessed as they are with conquest and showy heroics; a deeply restrained display etiquette (as compared with more established government-issued awards) due to the very personal nature of the individual achievements; and the rise of stretchy fabrics such as jersey and Lycra, informally worn by many bearers, which sag when burdened with one or more medals.

This book seeks to shine a long overdue spotlight on this rich and multifaceted field of interest. Gathered here are forty of the most important medals awarded in the search for true love, tracing the path from disenchantment and heartbreak to healing, romantic rebirth, and the universally happy ending of true love.

But even more than serving as an introduction to the artistry and splendor of romantic medals, it is hoped that this volume will further the original mission of Søren Linnæus and Edward George Goodwin: to recognize love as the glorious struggle that unites us all, and to reward those who risk their souls to seek it with all the pomp and circumstance they so richly deserve.

# LOVE MEDALS GLOSSARY
## WEAR THE FLAIR, TALK THE TALK

Throughout the history of awarding bravery in the search for true love with official awards and citations, a specific body of terminology and nomenclature has evolved around the practice. While lovers can simultaneously be linguistically ignorant and publicly celebrated, the ability to speak the language of love medals will only enhance one's opportunities for amatory honor.

AMOPHALERISTICS — The branch of numismatics (the study of coins, paper money, and other such tokens) dedicated to love medals and related romantic decorations. The term derives from *amare* (Latin, "to love") and *phalera*, a Roman military decoration often displayed on regimental standards or an infantryman's riding gear. An "amophalerist" is a person knowledgeable in amophaleristics.

AWARD — In its verb form, to give a medal of any kind in the pursuit of love. As a noun, the word indicates a certain type of medal, as in the Expert Vocalization Award for Confident Vowel Use in Adult Situations.

AXIAL DYSTONIA, HYPERLAUDATIAL (HAD) — Abnormal forward bending of the spine due to the quantity and weight of one's love medals (see fig. 01; see also "Rack"). HAD is exacerbated by the frequent patting of the bearer's back for his or her staggering romantic achievement. Starting in 1971, a special medal for HAD sufferers was awarded until its discontinuation in 1989 as a result of official recognition of the award's heavy irony.

*Fig. 01*

**CLASPS & CLUSTERS** — Acknowledgments of extenuating circumstances can be observed via the affixing of clasps, bars, clusters, or other such pins to the ribbon. Subsequent awards can also be recognized with a metal numeral affixed to the ribbon of the medal as initially issued.

**EFFIGY** — If the head of the lover is pictured on the medal, it is referred to as the "effigy" regardless of whether or not the recipient bears ill will toward the subject.

**ELIGIBILITY** — Some medals can only be awarded after certain outlined conditions have been met, such as duration of achievement, extraordinary acts of valor, or specifically stipulated meritorious conduct. Regulations document these criteria and spell out administration procedures.

**ENGRAVING** — To personalize the medal, certain facts can be engraved on the object's rim or reverse, such as the recipient's name, the date the award is given, and the date of the qualifying achievement (see also "Reverse").

**LONG SERVICE/GOOD CONDUCT MEDALS** — Given the difficulty of maintaining mutually healthy long-term love relationships, a dedicated category of medal is awarded to those who excel in duration and appropriate behavior over decades. Such medals are subject to predesignated "qualifying service."

**LOVE GONG** — Slang term for a love medal, initially referring only to the Order of the T. Rex for the Most Seductive Use of Platform Heels and Chest Hair (awarded from 1967 to 1977) but later understood to mean any love medal.

**MEDALOLUCIDATURAPHILIA** — Addiction to the smell of medal polish.

**MEDAL** — A cast metal object, generally in the shape of a disk, star, or cross, embossed or enameled with commemorative imagery, awarded to honor a particular and extraordinary action or accomplishment.

# LOVE MEDALS GLOSSARY
(CONTINUED)

OBVERSE—The front side of a medal (see also "Reverse").

ORDER OF WEAR—For the multiple-medal recipient, the sequence in which awards are to be arranged, by order of precedence (highest to the left, lowest to the right) along a medal bar for attachment to the recipient's clothing (see fig. 02-A; see also "Rack").

PEACOCK—One who wears a full rack of medals in daily life in a counter-productive attempt to display his or her (but usually his) romantic prowess, providing both too much information and a helpful character indication.

POSTNOMINAL LETTERS—To broadcast their honors, individuals may append to their full names acronymic letters of earned awards. For example, a recipient of the Worst-of-Times Medal for Breakup Survival can go by "John Doe, MBS."

RACK—An array of medals and ribbons arranged on a medal bar (see fig. 02-A), allowing the bearer to wear or display awards in one crisp unit instead of having to assemble them each time. Bearers are admonished to refrain from the obvious puns and double entendres (see fig. 02-B).

*Fig. 02-A*                    *Fig. 02-B*

**RESTRICTED WEAR**—The issuing body may stipulate that the medals are to be worn only on specified occasions, such as dates, or, conversely, may expressly *not* be worn on dates. Motivations for restricted wear include preventing the embarrassment of persons previously involved with the bearer; in such cases, the insignia may be worn at ceremonies or gatherings that include only other recipients of the same award (see also "Selective Display").

**REVERSE**—The rear surface of a medal, sometimes decorated but often left blank. The award's identifying details may be engraved on the reverse (see also "Engraving" and "Obverse").

**RIBBON**—Ribbons not only serve to hang medals for purposes of display (from a suspender ring or bar) but also identify the award with a distinctive and meaningful pairing. While all medals have an associated ribbon with a unique sequence of striped colors, not all ribbons correspond to a medal. For recipients of multiple medals, a narrow bar displaying only the ribbon of each medal is worn for ease and quietude (see fig. 02-A).

**SELECTIVE DISPLAY**—Medals that could cause personal embarrassment, betray the trust of one's partner, or come off as bragging may be displayed in their pin variant, worn on the inside of the bearer's lapel, to be flashed when appropriate or desired (see also "Restricted Wear").

**UNIT CITATION**—While individual citations honor single persons, unit citations recognize meritorious service by a romantic unit (generally consisting of two members) in a specific operation.

**VOYEUR**—An individual who collects medals but does not earn them.

**WARRANT**—A document that accompanies a love award, signed by the medal's issuing body, specifying the recipient, the reasons or occasion for the award's issuance, eligibility criteria, and any corresponding instructions or regulations. The warrant is not to be confused with an informal love letter.

Medal Registry No. L-01 | Family: Love | Category: Breakup

# The Shadow-of-a-Doubt Medal of Creeping Disenchantment

AWARDED FOR: **Recognizing the first tendrils of concern about the long-term viability of an outwardly healthy relationship, based on anything from long-ignored basic disagreements to an ever-growing sense of disillusionment.**

MEDAL: Slightly worn, almost imperceptibly tarnished gold, indicating impurity to the careful observer (pure gold, of course, doesn't tarnish) but appearing just fine to everybody else.

RIBBON: The amber color of autumn leaves flanked by encroaching stripes of snowy white.

ON REVERSE: "It's quiet ... too quiet."

RELATED AWARDS:

The Order of the Cursed Microscope for Highly Detailed Criticism

The Holmes Trophy for the Expert Reading of Subtle Clues

L'Ordre National de la Légion d'Ennui

The Golden Projector Award for Externalizing Your Own Fears and Misgivings

The Advanced Engineering Badge for Extraordinary Achievements in Molehill Expansion

"What makes you think we have a problem? We both work hard, that's all. But we're totally fine. Seriously. You think I should be worried? It's noticeable, isn't it?"
—*Steve Seyfried, 39, Los Angeles, California*

"I don't think that there's anything going on with us. Maybe. Yeah. I'm not sure. Ask me again in a month."
—*Jana Miller, 31, Canton, Ohio*

Medal Registry No. L-02 | Family: Love | Category: Breakup

# The Order of the Ostrich

AWARDED FOR: **Managing to ignore a mounting sense of disenchantment and foreboding in favor of convincing oneself that all is well in the relationship.**

MEDAL: Aluminum plated in pyrite (commonly known as fool's gold).

RIBBON: A wavy, rose-colored stripe flows down the center of a thunderhead gray ribbon, symbolizing the Nile, which ain't just a river in Egypt.

ON REVERSE: "Ignorantia beatitudo" (ignorance is bliss).

CLASPS & CLUSTERS: Brass Blinder Clusters are affixed to the ribbon for truly heroic feats of ignoring the unignorable, such as one's partner flirting with somebody else in one's presence, solo tropical vacations, and becoming a third wheel at one's own holiday party.

RELATED AWARDS:

The Brave-Face Medal for Selflessly Hiding Deep Despair

The "I Know You Are, But What Am I?" Citation for Aggressive Damage Control

The Cognitive Dissonance Badge with Alternate Reality Ribbon

The Soloist Star of Finding Solace in Single-Serving Foods and Activities

The Celtic Cross of Emotional Pretzel Logic

The Belated Realization of Complete Incompatibility Commendation

"It's much better now. We're just so exhausted most of the time. When we get time together, it's always great. Oh, and he told me about the girl you saw him with. They're friends from high school. It's nothing."

—*Brenda Snyder, 28, Sheridan, Wyoming*

# The Advanced Pragmatism Cross

**AWARDED FOR:** **Choosing the dull but ever-present pain of living in a loveless, dysfunctional relationship over the searing trauma of a breakup and the dispiriting return to singledom.**

**MEDAL:** An alloy of pewter and tin dipped in a thick layer of lead, which gives the medal its surprising heaviness and dull, scuffed finish.

**RIBBON:** Black stripes forever separated by an expanse of dark gray.

**ON REVERSE:** "I have nothing to offer but blood, toil, tears, and sweat. We have before us an ordeal of the most grievous kind." —Winston Churchill

**CLASPS & CLUSTERS:** A cheerfully enameled "Meh" clasp is awarded for reaching a state of Zen-like gallows humor.

**RELATED AWARDS:**

The Infinitely Delayed Gratification Medal

The Professional Achievement Award for the Most Voluntary Unpaid Overtime Hours

The Order of Silent Suffering and Stoic Endurance

The Great Sublimation Cross with New Puppy Clasp and a Renewed Interest in Painting

"When we go out to eat, I'll sometimes excuse myself, go to the restroom, and slowly bang my head against the stall door for a while. Actually feeling physical pain gives me comfort and gets me through the rest of the evening. And you know what? It's still better than being alone."

—Ben O'Neill, 48, Montauk, New York

MEDAL REGISTRY No. L-04 | FAMILY: Love | CATEGORY: Breakup

# The Pandering Star

**AWARDED FOR:** Saying and doing anything and everything in the hopes that a wave of compliments and goodwill can save—and maybe even reignite—a fizzling relationship.

**MEDAL:** Bright yellow gold, polished to a sparkling finish, with a few diamonds sprinkled in for good measure.

**RIBBON:** A purple ribbon, symbolizing the panderer's extravagant prose, embellished with a slavish pattern of golden fleurs de lis.

**ON REVERSE:** "If you're reading this, you're just too marvelous, too marvelous for words."

**CLASPS & CLUSTERS:** A Broken Spine Clasp is added upon surrender of one's most deeply held opinions and beliefs to aid the pandering effort.

**RELATED AWARDS:**

The Mercantile Expeditionary Medal with Forced-Smile Clasp for Outstanding Endurance in Search of New Garments

The Silver Tongue Award for Inventive and Effusive Praise

The "Just a Little Lower" Star for Selfless Massage Service

The Undaunted Shrug Medal for Perseverance Under Emotional Drought Conditions

The Dutch Legion of Honor "Dike Finger" Award for a Heroic Last-Ditch Effort

"I cut back on my food budget so I could bring her flowers every week and pretended I was fascinated to hear endlessly about the nuances of her choir group's social dynamics. I figured at some point she'd remember she loved me."
—*Brian Fugit, 27, San Antonio, Texas*

Medal Registry No. L-05 | Family: Love | Category: Breakup

# The Six-Month Involuntary Abstinence Cross

**AWARDED FOR:** Enduring a period of undesired celibacy (unrelated to medical issues) lasting six months or longer while in a committed relationship.

**MEDAL:** Originally minted from pure unobtainium but now issued in a quietly resigned alloy of aluminum and tin.

**RIBBON:** Yellow, bleached of hope by the merciless passage of time spent with nothing but memories and fantasies.

**ON REVERSE:** "Please, sir, I want some more." —*Oliver Twist*, Charles Dickens

**CLASPS & CLUSTERS:** Upon completion of the first six months of involuntary abstinence, a tin teardrop is affixed to the ribbon for each additional month. When those subsequent months add up to six, a leaden clasp is issued, inscribed "How long, oh Lord?"

**RELATED AWARDS:** The Collateral Damage Citation for Passive-Aggressive Conduct in the Workplace

The Verizon Broadband Customer of the Month Award

The Perfect Gym Attendance Award

The Solitaire Citation for Advances in the Field of Manual Relief (presented by Jergens)

"After going three months without making it past a half-hearted cuddle, I brought it up with my girlfriend, who said, 'Is that all I am to you? A convenient source for sex?'"
—*Scott Collins, 31, Beaver Creek, Alaska*

"Maybe he'd notice me if I made more of an effort to go along with what turns him on. Like, I could dress up as a resource-allocation report. If you'll excuse me, I'm going to go cry now."
—*Colleen Henley, 39, Tupelo, Mississippi*

# YOU DESERVE A LOVE MEDAL—SAYS WHO?

## THE COUNCIL OF ROMANTIC DECORATIONS

While love medals were not without precedent, following centuries of ad hoc honors (such as supportive amatory petraglyphs or a shared flagon of celebratory mead), the first set of official decorations for love and the governing body that would award them thereafter derive from the shared vision of a Swedish engineer and a British historian.

Following the end of a passionate but ultimately doomed five-year relationship with the daughter of his powerful employer, at the age of thirty-three, in 1867, the engineer Søren Linnæus fled his native Sweden, fearing professional reprisal for a breakup in which he was blameless. Linnæus set out for Victorian England to stake his claim in the Industrial Revolution and quickly established himself as a gifted designer of advanced steam engines. He subsequently started his own engineering concern and spent the next ten years registering dozens of lucrative patents.

As successful as he grew to be in his work, however, Linnæus remained hapless in matters of love. Despite his best efforts to attract a suitable mate, he was a stranger in his own time—too romantic and progressive in ways that startled more traditional souls, and too much an engineer to connect with the high-minded socialites open to his liberal ideas. To soothe his loneliness and remain engaged in the world, Linnæus established a salon of like minds that met fortnightly at the Reform Club, inviting notable voices drawn from science, the humanities, and the culture at large. Oscar Wilde described the gatherings as "charming, and only rarely tedious." It is here that Linnæus first met the historian Edward George Goodwin.

Goodwin had established himself as a prodigy with his research into the history of British chivalry, dating to tenth-century France, and was later elevated to Assistant Provost of Worcester College, Oxford. Goodwin found a kindred spirit in Linnæus—he too had achieved his professional success at the expense of his personal life.

In the context of an extensive discussion of their recent romantic misfortunes, Goodwin looked at Linnæus one evening and uttered the fateful words: "You deserve a medal." The moment would later be remembered by both men as meaningful. It was Linnæus who then took the idea to its rightful conclusion and had the first Worst-of-Times Medal for Breakup Survival crafted as a consolation gift for Goodwin. Goodwin quickly repaid the favor with a Bait-and-Switch Cross for Eluding One's Chaperone (since discontinued) and upped the ante by enclosing a detailed set of rules and regulations for the award's issuance.

Out of their pleasure in these ether-fueled, idiosyncratic and deeply personal fancies, both men determined there was a true need for awards in this most human of endeavors and decided to establish the Council of Romantic Decorations. By now a man of great means, Linnæus acquired offices in the Guildhall of Chipping Wycombe, halfway between London and Oxford, hired staff, and set up a sizable endowment to provide for the manufacture and administration of the medals in perpetuity. Goodwin, in turn, used his position in academia to gather the brightest, most compassionate minds of the time to serve as the inaugural dozen guides of this new institution, the Council of Twelve.

Established in 1894, the council drew up the inaugural list of medals, everything from Finding Love Outside Your Social Class to Wedded Bliss in Foreign Territories. They also established the way medals are still awarded today: friends or partners of the nominee petition the council by outlining noteworthy achievements and references (for the nomination form, see page 112). After vetting by assistant council members, the Council of Twelve makes the final determination based on personal merit, valor, and chivalry.

Once minted, the award is sent to the person who submitted the original nomination so that he or she may be the one to present it; it was the opinion of Linnæus and Goodwin that the medals should recognize not just the many achievements large and small that lead toward the goal of true love, but also the bonds that form among friends along the way.

*Søren Linnæus and
Edward George Goodwin, 1905*

Medal Registry No. L-06 | Family: Love | Category: Breakup

# The Worst-of-Times Medal for Breakup Survival

**AWARDED FOR:** Experiencing the universally excruciating demise of a once-cherished relationship.

**MEDAL:** Badly corroded copper with multiple scuffs, cuts, and abrasions, with a jagged crack spreading from the center bottom to the heart of the medal.

**RIBBON:** Black and blue.

**ON REVERSE:** "Better a painful end than unending pain."

**CLASPS & CLUSTERS:** Clasps are issued with the name of each ex and the birth and death dates of the respective relationships. Rusty steel daggers are affixed to the ribbon if the breakup resulted from betrayal.

**RELATED AWARDS:** The Cascade Failure Cross for Sudden and Total Relationship Unravelment

The Charlton Heston Medal for Dramatically Falling to Your Knees and Pounding the Ground with Your Fists

The Nervous Breakdown Cross with Panic Clusters

The Friendly Breakup Award (established by act of law, yet never awarded)

"We both tried hard to make it work. But then she stopped, and I did, too. It took us another year to finally call it quits. Don't underestimate the force of habit. That last year was more painful than anything before or since."
—*Eva Stewart, 32, Lenexa, Kansas*

"'What doesn't kill you makes you stronger.' What a crock."
—*Jackson Moorstead, 51, Amagansett, New York*

MEDAL REGISTRY No. L-07 | FAMILY: Love | CATEGORY: Breakup

# The Exceptional Courage Badge for Enduring the First Day After

**AWARDED FOR:** **Living through the first devastatingly empty day following the end of a long-term relationship.**

**MEDAL:** Half-inch-thick lead, symbolizing a heart shielded from post-nuclear radiation and fallout.

**RIBBON:** A scorched gray ribbon with frayed borders of deepest black and a single strand of coagulated red woven dead center.

**ON REVERSE:** "After all . . . tomorrow is another day." —Scarlett O'Hara, *Gone with the Wind*

**CLASPS & CLUSTERS:** Shriveled heart pins are affixed to the ribbon in recognition of subsequent first days after.

**RELATED AWARDS:**

The Our Lady of Blessed Catatonia Medal

The Friend-in-Need Star for Immediate Post-Traumatic Care

The Ursa Major Citation for Thirty-Six Hours of Bed Rest

The *Law & Order* Marathon TV Appreciation Badge

The Imminent Deadline Salvation Medal for Well-Timed Professional Distractions

The Order of the Emergency Danish for Judicious Self-Medication

"Now that I look back on it, I'd rather have my wisdom teeth pulled without anesthesia than go through that day again."
—*Andy Spiegel, 35, Sioux City, Iowa*

"Once the air rushes out of the ship and into deep space, you realize it's not the explosion that'll kill you."
—*Karen O'Duffy, 44, San Diego, California*

THE SEPARATION OF COLLECTIONS

COMMENDATION

MEDAL REGISTRY No. L-08 | FAMILY: Love | CATEGORY: Breakup

# The Separation of Collections Commendation

**AWARDED FOR:** **Completing the harrowing process of negotiating the post-relationship division of property.**

**MEDAL:** Stainless steel perforated down the center.

**RIBBON:** Forty parallel vertical stripes of various colors, separated at the center by a thick dotted line that continues the perforation of the medal itself.

**ON REVERSE:** "This medal belongs to _____."

**CLASPS & CLUSTERS:** A Solomonic halved-baby pin in silver is awarded for the selfless surrender of deeply personal items acquired together and desired by both parties.

**RELATED AWARDS:**

The Changed iTunes Password Citation for Reestablished Electronic Boundaries

The Bent Wookiee Cross of Accidental Damage and Loss

The "We'll Always Have Ferris" Surrendered DVD Replacement Medal

The Unfriending UnFacebook Unmedal

The Leon Trotsky Medal for the Necessary Retouching or Resection of Joint Photos

The Bittersweet Symphony Badge for Negotiating the Use of Remaining Season Tickets

"This was the first time since the breakup that I'd spent time in the same room with my ex, and it was tough. We both wanted the blanket we bought in Peru to take stargazing at night, but he was nice enough to give it up. Weirdly, though, what hurt most were the things neither of us wanted."

—*Jennifer Benjamin, 28, Chicago, Illinois*

Medal Registry No. L-09 | Family: Love | Category: Breakup

# The Sanity Award for Escaping the Breakup-Makeup Cycle

**AWARDED FOR:** Finally and definitively ending the repetitive, emotionally fraught process of temporarily reuniting to experience once again the fleeting sense of physical and emotional belonging, or merely to have sex.

**MEDAL:** Stamped from a bimetallic strip of steel and copper that bends according to the wearer's fluctuating body temperature.

**RIBBON:** Dupioni silk appearing bright pink from one angle and dark blue from another.

**ON REVERSE:** Around the medal's perimeter, "I will not make this mistake again. I will not make this mistake again. I will not make this mistake again."

**RELATED AWARDS:** The Voice-of-Sanity Medal for Valorous Telling of Truth to a Benighted Comrade

The Unclouded Vision Star for Thinking with Your Head

The Bygone Cross of Putting the Past Where It Belongs

The Crazy Sexy Uncool Medal for Realizing the Difference Between Allure and Insanity

The Quantum-Leap Cross for Successfully Shifted Paradigms

The Pop-Pop-Pop Commendation for Active Suction Cup Disengagement

"It's like a drug—just one more hit. Every time I think, 'Okay, that was the last one.' But it's just so easy to fall back into our old rhythms. And there's stuff I like that's embarrassing to explain to somebody new. But hell—peacock feathers or no, this has to end!"

—*Henry Simmons, 31, Grand Forks, North Dakota*

THE LONG HARD STARE MEDAL

OF PERSONAL FAILURE IN LOVE

MEDAL REGISTRY No. L-10 | FAMILY: Love | CATEGORY: Breakup

# The Long Hard Stare Medal of Personal Failure in Love

AWARDED FOR: **Reaching the sobering conclusion that the common element uniting the romantic failures comprising one's love life is oneself, and realizing that one is thus neither ready for nor worthy of true love.**

MEDAL: Unblinking stainless steel.

RIBBON: A laserlike construction-worker-orange stripe cuts sharply through a field of foggy gray.

ON REVERSE: "Truth is like the sun. You can shut it out for a time, but it ain't goin' away." —Elvis Presley

CLASPS & CLUSTERS: Sharpened steel thorns pierce the back of the ribbon, lacerating the front, to commemorate especially painful insights about recent behavior or mortifying chagrin at the belated recognition of mistakes long past.

RELATED AWARDS:

The Self-Recrimination Cross with Thorn Garter

The Tragic Heroism Star for Successful Internal Rebranding

The Reflexive Pessimism Badge with Probable-Lonely-Death Clasp

The Kernel of Truth Cross with Balanced-Appraisal Cluster

The Möbius Medal of Recursive Logic

"Let's face it: My love life has been a series of failures, ranging from uninspired fizzles to epic, teeth-rattling disasters, culminating in this latest, greatest romantic catastrophe. I'd love to blame . . . you know . . . *them*, but who am I kidding?"
—*Kirstin Hardwick, 42, Rochester, New York*

The Surviving Our First Winter Together Medal with Stored Berries and Dried Mammoth-Meat Strips

The Order of Writing Each Other's Name in the Sand of the Valley of Kings

The Pheasant Feather Cross for Finding Love at a Senatorial Orgy

The Mary Magdalene Star for Dating Way Out of Your League

The Mead Hall Commendation with Seal Fur and Horns for Surviving a Viking Vacation Fling

The Syphilis Avoidance Citation

The Covering Up Your Suitor's Heresy Cross with Golden Halo and Backup Cross

The Shameless Ankle Revelation Citation

15,000 BCE

2,000 BCE

50 BCE

30 CE

970 CE

1494 CE

1633 CE

1670 CE

# DATING MEDALS OF YESTERYEAR

## A LOOK BACK AT HONORS THAT HAVE COME AND GONE

While love may make the heart skip many a beat, it cannot stop the flow of time. Over the years, the pursuit of love has taken many forms, some of which seem strange to the modern eye, but rest assured they were the Unlimited Texting Cross for Stellar Love Notes in 160 Characters or Less of their day.

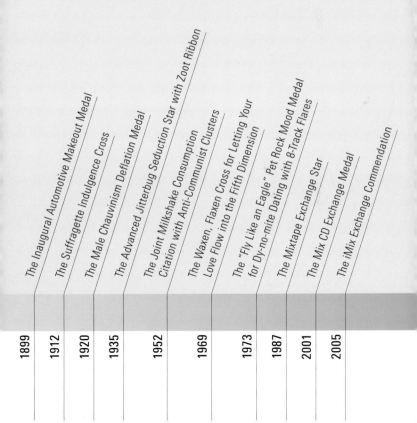

|  |  |
|------|-------|
| 1899 | The Inaugural Automotive Makeout Medal |
| 1912 | The Suffragette Indulgence Cross |
| 1920 | The Male Chauvinism Deflation Medal |
| 1935 | The Advanced Jitterbug Seduction Star with Zoot Ribbon |
| 1952 | The Joint Milkshake Consumption Citation with Anti-Communist Clusters |
| 1969 | The Waxen, Flaxen Cross for Letting Your Love Flow into the Fifth Dimension |
| 1973 | The "Fly Like an Eagle" Pet Rock Mood Medal for Dy-no-mite Dating with 8-Track Flares |
| 1987 | The Mixtape Exchange Star |
| 2001 | The Mix CD Exchange Medal |
| 2005 | The iMix Exchange Commendation |

THE ORDER OF THE GOLDEN PINT
FOR BRAVERY IN THE FACE OF SORROW

# The Order of the Golden Pint for Bravery in the Face of Sorrow

AWARDED FOR: **Making it through the lonely, haunting bursts of mourning in the months following your breakup, after friends and family have exhausted their reservoirs of compassion.**

MEDAL: Soft white gold.

RIBBON: Butterscotch ribbon with a center swirl of chocolate and raspberry.

ON REVERSE: "Here bring your wounded hearts, here tell your anguish; Earth has no sorrow that [ice cream] cannot heal." —Thomas Moore

CLASPS & CLUSTERS: Golden sprinkles are added for coping with emotional downturns by means of particularly inventive acts of caloric bravery, such as dipping deep-fried Snickers bars into partially melted rocky road ice cream then eating them s'mores-style while lying in the fetal position.

RELATED AWARDS: The Grand Self-Soothing Cross with Binky Ribbon

The Involuntary Phil Collins Appreciation Cross

The Wallow-in-Misery Medal with Drawn Shades and Disabled Phone

The Overcompensation Citation for Excessive Cardiovascular Exercise Following Emotional Weight Gain

"Oh God . . . I thought I was past bursting into tears at any insurance commercial with a string section. Still? Great. Because now I can mix it up between being sad, being embarrassed about being sad, and being pissed that I have to be embarrassed that I'm sad. Where the hell did my spoon go?"
—*Joely Madison, 25, Yakima, Washington*

Medal Registry No. L-12 | Family: Love | Category: Breakup

# The Mutual Friends Diplomacy Award

AWARDED FOR: **Swallowing one's understandable and considerable anger, gritting one's teeth, and making nice with one's ex to maintain the connection with mutual friends who inexplicably refuse to pick a side.**

MEDAL: Heavily tarnished silver.

RIBBON: Jaundiced yellow bisected by bands of emerald green (to symbolize jealousy) and crimson (to represent barely contained rage).

ON REVERSE: "Yes, it's nice to see you, too."

CLASPS & CLUSTERS: A special tin dove pin is attached to the ribbon for forgiving friends who have chosen to side with your ex.

RELATED AWARDS:

The Henry Kissinger Realpolitik Cross of Bitter Compromise

The Tabula Rasa Star for Decisive Acquisition of All New Friends

The Polar Bear Citation for Hiding Your True Feelings Behind an Inscrutable Mask and Then Killing a Poor Little Penguin for No Apparent Reason

The "What'd I Tell You?" Vindication Medal for Regaining Errant Friends Due to Belatedly Revealed Ex Craziness

"When John and I got together I had just joined the American Institute of Model Railroad Enthusiasts, so naturally I brought him along to all our events. Now that we're no longer a couple, a lot of those people insist on still being friends with him. Why? John wouldn't know an HO-scale bus stop from a G-scale mailbox! I hope the soldering on their command stations corrodes."

—*Roger Marsden, 46, Eau Claire, Wisconsin*

MEDAL REGISTRY No. L-13 | FAMILY: Love | CATEGORY: Singlehood

# The Post-Relationship Hibernation Cross

AWARDED FOR: **Resisting the urge to leap immediately into the dating pool following a breakup (to soothe the ego or distract the mind) in favor of experiencing a fallow period of romantic inactivity intended to reset the emotional compass, regain strength, and allow healing to take place.**

MEDAL: Lustrous but inert tungsten, which easily and appropriately turns brittle if it contains even small impurities.

RIBBON: Soft, comfortable, forgiving gray heather jersey flanked by nonjudgmental elastic borders.

ON REVERSE: "The best of all medicines are resting and fasting." —Benjamin Franklin

RELATED AWARDS: The Medal of Blessed and Enlightened Solitude

The Best Friends Forever (Again) Medal for Reaching Out to Long-Lost Pals

The Advanced Gardening Cross with New Ivy Lattice

The "You'll Find It When You're Not Looking" Demerit for Feigned Hibernation

"At first I wanted to start dating again right away, but I was just too exhausted from all the drama. And then it hit me: this is my window to gain a few extra pounds that nobody will have to see sans clothing! This is my time to read books, catch up on the movies I missed, and converse with friends without crying into their drinks about my epic misery. *They* deserve a break, too!"

—*Lynne Jeffries, 33, Cambridge, Massachusetts*

THE SELF-RESPECT

ME

RECOVERY STAR

Medal Registry No. L-14 | Family: Love | Category: Singlehood

# The Self-Respect Recovery Star

**AWARDED FOR:** **Successfully calming the alternating waves of despair and euphoria that follow a failed relationship and moving into a stable state of enlightened self-respect stemming from hard-earned self-awareness.**

**MEDAL:** Pure gold surrounding a tough core of solid platinum.

**RIBBON:** Flanking optimistic sky blue are verdant stripes of rich green, symbolizing the fresh growth of insight and strength.

**ON REVERSE:** "Per aspera ad astra" (through adversity to the stars).

**CLASPS & CLUSTERS:** A gold carpenter's-level clasp (featuring an actual level) is added to the ribbon for maintaining one's equanimity through fresh setbacks or unexpected run-ins with one's ex.

**RELATED AWARDS:**

The Compressed Bounceback Medal for Reduced Emotional Recovery Time

The Renewed Optimism Citation with Expanded Horizon Clasp

The Straightened Spine Star with Bronze Spring in the Step

The Once-More-with-Feeling Cross of Sexual Variety

"Oh Lord, I was such a mess. I'm embarrassed to even remember the endless tearful phone calls and convoluted emails to my friends, the weepy late-night confessionals while hunched over coffee and sandwiches at the diner. I hope that I'll be as good a friend to them as they've been to me. Then again, I hope I won't have to be. All that emotion … I think I still have some on my shoes."

—*Frank Albers, 47, Kirksville, Missouri*

THE LEARNED OPTIMISM SPEAR

# The Learned
# Optimism Star

**AWARDED FOR:** **Completion of the tenth self-help book in pursuit of wisdom to be applied to future relationships.**

**MEDAL:** Highly buffed brass.

**RIBBON:** Optimistic rose with a bold center bar of passionate red, framed by streaks of sunrise orange.

**ON REVERSE:** "We ask ourselves, Who am I to be brilliant, gorgeous, talented, fabulous? Actually, who are you not to be?"
—Marianne Williamson

**CLASPS & CLUSTERS:** A brass thumbs-up is added to the ribbon for each completed self-help book or seminar beyond the original ten, making for an increasingly festive presentation of personal growth and serving as a progressive reminder of one's intrinsic okayness.

**RELATED AWARDS:** The Most Exalted Order of the Oprah Poobah

The Secret Medal of Manifestly Destined Manifest Destiny

The Anthony Robbins Medal for Awakening the Giant Within

The Kundalini Cross for Achievements in Advanced Chakra Realignment

The Golden Navel Observation Citation

"Of course my life was messed up! My karmic matrix was all over the place. My priority pyramid was a shambles. But now I've got a plan, I've got a system, and I have a huge antioxidant shake every morning. I'm manifesting good things and good things will happen to me. Do you have any plans for dinner?"
—*Jason Kinsella, 34, Venice, California*

# HENRY VIII
## Monarch, Legal and Religious Innovator

1. The Royal Order of the Hopeless Romantic

2. The Grand Overcompensation Star for Dealing with Issues of Infertility

3. The Papal Order of Faithful Adherence to God's Laws of Holy Matrimony

4. The Ingenuity Star for Changing the Rules of the Game of Love

5. The Archbishop of Canterbury Medal for creating the Archdiocese of Canterbury

6. The "New Cross" Cross for Advancements in the Field of Organized Religion

7. The Clean Break Star for Permanently Severing Ties With One's Ex (issued 4 times)

8. The Anne Boleyn Medal for Finding Love Right Under One's Nose

9. The "Where Was My Head?" Medal for Not Being Afraid to Change One's Mind About One's Partner

10. The Order of the Insatiable Appetite for Wantonly Indulging in Pleasures of the Flesh

11. The Serial Dater's Medal for Finding One's Groove

12. The Saintly Patience Medal for Not Letting Every Argument About Religion End in Your Wife's Decapitation

13. The "All's Well that Ends Well" Cross for Letting One's Kids Overcompensate for One's Profligate Ways (posthumous, not shown)

# GREAT RACKS IN HISTORY
## MEDALS OF THE FAMOUS AND INFAMOUS

To the trained eye, a full rack of medals reads like a résumé, or, in notorious cases such as these, like a tragic saga. In either case, a glorious narrative of humanity is conveyed merely through the coordination of accessories.

## JENNIFER CRANSTON
### Bennigan's Night Manager

1. The Debatable Choice Badge for Dropping Out of College and Moving to a New Town for Love

2. The Adjusted Expectations Medal for Having to Take a Job You Already Had in High School

3. The Entirely Expected Plot-Twist Citation for Finding Out Your Partner Isn't Right for You After All

4. The Order of the Weary Sigh for Surviving Unsolicited Come-Ons

5. The Medal of Bitter Lessons Learned for Accepting Unsolicited Come-Ons

6. The Drowning-Your-Sorrows Star for Eating Customers' Leftover French Fries

7. The Doris Day Commendation for Singing "Happy Birthday" As If for the First Time

8. The Trenches Medal for Bonding with Your Lookalike Co-Workers

9. The Best Use of Free Top-Shelf Liquor Star for Sleeping with a Visiting Division Manager Without Removal of Suspenders

10. The Point-of-Pride Medal for Never Getting Docked for Inadequate Display of Flair

11. The New Tomorrows Pin for Returning to School

Medal Registry No. L-16 | Family: Love | Category: Singlehood

# The Silver Lining Cross for a Successful Rebound Fling

AWARDED FOR: **Successful completion of a low-stakes physical encounter in the wake of a failed relationship. This may include anything from a one-night stand with a stranger to a brief relationship with a colleague.**

MEDAL: Sterling silver (unsurprisingly).

RIBBON: Five parallel flirty stripes of light and dark lavender with tasteful but frisky black lace trim.

ON REVERSE: "Why yes, I'd love a nightcap!"

CLASPS & CLUSTERS: A Double-Down Silver Star of Exceptional Daring is affixed to the ribbon if the rebound fling involves public nudity, theme parks, or a neighbor.

RELATED AWARDS:

The Prometheus Award for Playing with Fire

The Order of the Big Dipper for Best Use of Company Ink

The Vegas Cross with Reality Suspension Clusters

The "John Smith" Single-Use Identity Medal

The Sex, Drugs, and Rock 'n' Roll Medal for Personal Achievements in Debauchery

The "Here's Looking at You" Citation for Alcoholic Optometry

The Walk-of-Shame Cross with Tousled Hair and Sunglasses

The Order of the Giant Sigh of Relief for Reliable Birth Control

"Thank you, Regional Conference for Distributed Computing and Network Administration—I am reborn!"
—*Peter Scofield, 45, La Jolla, California*

Medal Registry No. L-17 | Family: Love | Category: Singlehood

# The Persistent Online Dating Campaign Medal

**AWARDED FOR:** **Engaging in a sustained effort of online dating across multiple sites for a period of at least one year.**

**MEDAL:** Three-dimensional heart fashioned from silicon and adorned with gold circuit wiring.

**RIBBON:** Circuit-board green bisected by three broad vertical stripes of blue (Macintosh), penguin black (Linux), and green (Windows Vista).

**ON REVERSE:** "By choosing 'Accept Medal,' I certify I am at least 18 years old and agree to this medal's privacy policy and terms of use."

**CLASPS & CLUSTERS:** For every 50 people contacted online, a pixelated red enamel heart is affixed to the ribbon; for every 50 answered emails, a green heart; and for every 25 first dates completed, a gold heart.

**RELATED AWARDS:** The Truth-in-Advertising Medal for Stating Your Correct Height, Weight, and Age

The Razzle-Dazzle Cross for Posting Misleadingly Attractive Photos

The Shackleton Star for Searching Beyond the 25-Mile Limit

The "There, They're, and Their" Orthographic Charity Citation for Dating the Grammatically Impaired

"At this point, I don't even know how to react if somebody asks me out in the real world anymore. How old are you? Do you want kids? Who did you vote for? What's your favorite book? How can I know if we'd be a good match unless I have some information?"
—*Kim Davis, AKA HoneyBun1978, 33, Portland, Oregon*

"You looked taller in your pictures."
—*Sandy Pensom, AKA UniversLightCond, 45, Eagle Rock, California*

Medal Registry No. L-18 | Family: Love | Category: Singlehood

# The High-Wire Award for Forging a Friends-with-Benefits Arrangement

**AWARDED FOR:** Managing to establish and maintain intermittent sexual contact with another human being for the purpose of mutual physical enjoyment, while maintaining a safe, commitment-free emotional distance.

**MEDAL:** Light aluminum with a protective Teflon coating; attached to the bearer's chest not with the traditional pin, but with a hidden patch of Velcro.

**RIBBON:** Everyday beige shot through with playful, fiery threads of cherry red, deep purple, and hot pink.

**ON REVERSE:** "You home?"

**RELATED AWARDS:**

The Flying Wallenda Delicate Balance Cross

The Emotional Self-Discipline Star

The Energizer Bunny Rapid Mobilization Medal

The Awkward Real-World Encounter in the Presence of Friends Commendation

The Peaceful Transition to Friends-Without-Benefits Medal

"This is the perfect relationship! It's all of the good and none of the bad! I hope this lasts forever!"
—*Shane McCune, 31, Trenton, New Jersey*

"I really like him. I'm sure he'll realize I'm the one for him after we've been having no-commitment sex for a while."
—*Sadie Hewitt, 31, Trenton, New Jersey*

Medal Registry No. L-19 | Family: Love | Category: Singlehood

# The Butterfly Order of the Unexpected Crush

**AWARDED FOR:** Silencing the inner critic to allow oneself to fall instantly head over heels in love when presented with somebody undeniably delicious.

**MEDAL:** Solid gold, in the shape of a butterfly, decorated with bright enamel accents and emblazoned with two small, hopeful diamonds.

**RIBBON:** Springtime green framed by cloudlike white borders, vertically bisected by a vibrant side-to-side sine wave of bright pink, symbolizing the boundless energy of young love.

**ON REVERSE:** Around the medal's perimeter, "You're the cutest! No, *you're* the cutest. *You're* the cutest! No, *you're* the cutest."

**CLASPS & CLUSTERS:** Should the unexpected crush occur between previously platonic friends, a gold cluster depicting two playing puppy dogs is added.

**RELATED AWARDS:** The "Music Be the Food of Love" Golden Mixtape Award

The All-Too-Temporary Perfection Star

The Slow-Motion-Running Airport Hug Medal

The Reluctant Return to Reality Commendation

"When a friend set me up with Kim, I actually considered canceling. I was tired and didn't expect anything but the eighty-seventh *Groundhog Day* first-date repeat. Well, it took me about ten seconds to feel like I was back in high school. My ears must've been the color of a fire engine."
—*Jim Gant, 39, Vail, Colorado*

# The Gallantry Cross

**AWARDED FOR:** **Consistently and graciously adhering to a chivalrous code of courtship conduct.**

---

**MEDAL:** Awarded in bronze (opening doors, pulling out chairs, laughing at mediocre jokes), silver (paying for dinner *and* a show, observing "ladies first" to a fault), or gold (heroic gestures above and beyond the call of duty).

**RIBBON:** Impeccable medium gray Super 150 wool with restrained green and purple pinstripes.

**ON REVERSE:** "After you, please."

**CLASPS & CLUSTERS:** A matte silver clasp is added to the ribbon for extraordinary acts of gallantry exceeding even the gold standard, such as offering oneself as a distraction to attacking bears or agreeing to a repeat Cirque du Soleil show.

---

**RELATED AWARDS:**

| | |
|---|---|
| The Common Courtesy Award for Proof-Reading You Emails | The Perfect Grace Medal for Bearing the Boorish |
| The Order of the Politely Deactivated BlackBerry | The "Death to the Dutch" Medal of Old-Fashioned Gastroeconomic Unilateralism |

"I work in accounts payable, so I don't get to be James Bond— please let me pull out your chair and pick up the tab."
—*Jeff Corke, 32, Toluca Lake, California*

"It wasn't all Tracy and Hepburn back then. Yes, equality is sexier than anything, but having somebody hold the door open for you or helping you into your coat? Why deprive yourself?"
—*Millicent Porter, 78, New York, New York*

# FOOL ME ONCE

## A GUIDE TO SPOTTING FALSE MEDALS

As long as there have been medals awarded in the pursuit of love, so have forgers created counterfeits and imposters fabricated fictitious medals. While some forgeries are obvious and easy to detect, others are more subtle. The informed collector will, as in love, always have the upper hand.

## PHYSICAL INDICATIONS OF AMOPHALERISTIC FORGERY

All medals should be checked against *Hetzer's Love Medal Companion*, the amophaleristics guide of record. Is the medal the correct diameter? Are the ribbon's stripes properly spaced? This inspection will expose most forgeries.

If identifying information such as the bearer's name or date of issue is engraved on the medal, compare it to the official register housed at the Carey Institute at the Library of Congress, which will also list any officially issued replacements.

Poor craftmanship such as soft edges and details (as seen in badly executed typography and unsightly background pebbling, for example) are a frequent indication of forgery.

Genuine medal ribbons are woven into stripes from differently dyed thread rather than printed on preassembled material. Printed ribbons exhibit fuzzy—not to mention one-sided—transitions between stripes.

Official medals never feature a portrait of the bearer—particularly one adhered with Elmer's Glue.

Some forgers attempt to alter existing medals—for example, by scratching out official typography and replacing it with hand-lettering. If any aspect of the medal does not look original, suspicions should be raised.

The most basic forgeries can be identified by inappropriate material choices. No paper medals have ever been issued, for example. Other material telltales include tablecloth ribbons, paperclip medal suspensions, and ribbon stripes drawn with a Sharpie.

Much can be told about a medal simply by dipping it into water. Genuine medals will have greater displacement than forgeries. They will also resist discoloration of medal or ribbon. If a medal dissolves in effervescent bubbles, it was likely carved from an Alka-Seltzer tablet.

Confirm that the medal's suspension mechanism matches official specifications and recorded samples. While forgers put great effort into the medal and ribbon, many cut corners on the suspension ring and mount. Check design, ring diameter, and materials used.

Always ascertain that the edge of the medal has the correct detailing (as specified in *Hetzer's*) and determine that it was crisply executed. Forged medals can often be identified by blunt, mismatched, or even absent edgework.

## THEMATIC INDICATIONS OF FORGERY

Real medals do not incorporate the bearer's name in the title. The Jane Carmichael Medal for Excellent First-Date Poise, for example, does not exist.

Beware of medals that provide all-too-convenient evidence against current accusations. A Medal for Being a Selfless Caretaker should be considered with suspicion when produced just as the bearer is being confronted about going AWOL during his or her partner's recent bout of stomach flu.

Be alert for medals that address an achievement that is overly specific to the bearer. The Romantic Achievement Award for Always Knowing the Perfect *Simpsons* Quote for the Occasion is almost certainly a fabrication.

Medals praising physical appearance and individual features are a particular favorite among forgers, motivated to overcompensate for feelings of inadequacy. No Order of Staggering Manliness was ever issued, nor a Perky Twins Star with C-Cup Clusters.

Medals in the pursuit of love honor the elative but not the superlative; forgers, by contrast, frequently get greedy. Thus a Great Kisser's Star may be real, but the Greatest Kisser's Star most likely is not.

Please note that personalized, handmade medals can only be considered forgeries if they are presented with the intent to deceive. When given as custom-made gifts, they can be extremely sweet and romantic, and as such have the full support and blessing of the relevant authorities.

Medal Registry No. L-21 | Family: Love | Category: Singlehood

# The First-Kiss Star

AWARDED FOR: **Meritorious and outstanding effort leading to the exchange of a mutually delightful first kiss.**

MEDAL: Minted from lustrous tantalum, representing the many-splendored sensations of initial lip-to-lip-to-lip-to-lip interaction.

RIBBON: Iridescent pink overlaid with ruby red rays that continue and extend the medal's perimeter rays (because the power of the first kiss cannot be contained by mere metal).

ON REVERSE: "A kiss is a lovely trick designed by nature to stop speech when words become superfluous." —Ingrid Bergman

CLASPS & CLUSTERS: Shiny Heart Clusters and Rainbow Pins are attached to each ribbon out of sheer exuberance. No further action is required on the part of the bearer.

RELATED AWARDS:

The "Everything's Different" Medal of Suddenly Changed Perspective

The Nikola Tesla Commendation for Massive Spark Generation

The Springtime Star of Reawakened Passions

The "Pop Goes My Heart" Medal for Sudden Love Song Susceptibility

The Romantic Fool Medal for Foolish Romanticism and Romantic Foolishness

The Tiny Tim Citation for Successfully Tiptoed Tulips

"When it actually happens, you have an instant of fear. 'Is it going to be good?' And then it *is* good, and the voice in your head finally shuts off, and everything's just right. It's better than anything!"

—Mary Shipman, 25, Long Beach, California

THE LEGION OF SAINTLY PATIENCE

FOR WAITING BY THE PHONE

# The Legion of Saintly Patience for Waiting by the Phone

**AWARDED FOR:** Maintaining a good-natured air of calm in the face of a return call delayed for longer than twenty-four hours following a romantic interaction.

**MEDAL:** Carved from soft, golden brown butternut wood (*Juglans cinerea*) and worried smooth by a thousand anxious turns in the hand.

**RIBBON:** For obsessive counting during idle hours, multiple pinstripes (18 yellow, 10 red, 23 blue, 21 green, and 28 white) flank a center half-inch stripe of silent black.

**ON REVERSE:** "Hello?! What? No, I'm happy with my long-distance plan."

**CLASPS & CLUSTERS:** A bronze Janus-head pin is added to the ribbon for enduring silences longer than seven days then responding to reestablished contact with convincingly feigned good cheer.

**RELATED AWARDS:**

The Advanced Mountaineering Star for Climbing the Walls

The Relentless Post-Date Self-Analysis Cross

The Order of Suspended Disbelief for Waiting Beyond Reason

The Self-Empowerment Medal for Crossing Gender-Normative Boundaries and Calling First

The Commendation of Restraint for Leaving Non-Needy Voicemails

The Red-Faced Chagrin Cross for Coming Off as Desperate

"I was sure my cell phone was broken. I repeatedly rang it from my office line just to make sure. When he finally called, it took me a few minutes to catch my breath. Too bad he turned out to be such a dufus on our second date. I had to duck his calls after that."

—*Cindy Mulke, 49, Grants Pass, Oregon*

Medal Registry No. L-23 | Family: Love | Category: Singlehood

# The Unlimited Texting Cross for Stellar Love Notes in 160 Characters or Less

**AWARDED FOR:** Consistent excellence in the realm of artfully abbreviated billets-doux delivered by means of text messaging.

**MEDAL:** Forged from columbite and tantalite ore, commonly known as coltan, mined in Australia.

**RIBBON:** Stylish matte silver bordered by even more stylish black, bisected by five parallel electric blue stripes symbolizing the network generations of 1G through 5G.

**ON REVERSE:** "You autocomplete me. #crush"

**CLASPS & CLUSTERS:** While no clasps or clusters are issued for the Unlimited Texting Cross, a selection of the bearer's best text messages are stored on the medal's SIM card.

**RELATED AWARDS:**

The Two-Day Loss of Battery Power Feeble-Excuse Badge

The Texting-to-a-Landline Epic Fail Citation

The Future-Is-Now Star for Proposing Marriage via Text Message

The Minute of Static Cross for Accidentally Pocket-Dialed Calls

The Irving Penn Medal of Achievement in Cell Phone Photography

The "I Knve Ynt So Mnch?" Drunk Texting Cross

The Indiscreet Sexting Star with Forwarding Clusters

"Harry is an alphanumeric Byron. When my phone chimes, the world stops and my heart sings."
—*Sharon Calvert, 82, Carpinteria, California*

Medal Registry No. L-24 | Family: Love | Category: Singlehood

# The Medal of Making Out

**AWARDED FOR:** **The spirited and sustained pursuit of physical contact with a partner by means of hugging, kissing, caressing, cuddling, fondling, hugging, necking, petting, smooching, and/or snuggling.**

**MEDAL:** Issued in bronze (first base), silver (second base), or gold (third base), but always covered in a slight mist of perspiration.

**RIBBON:** Hastily assembled from several slightly rumpled fabrics of random color and texture that have been cursorily smoothed out to pass post-canoodle inspection.

**ON REVERSE:** "Baby we can talk all night, but that ain't gettin' us nowhere."
—Meat Loaf

**CLASPS & CLUSTERS:** Location-specific brass clusters are awarded as warranted. The eleven most frequently issued are (in descending order): couch, car, movie theater, classroom, planetarium, tent, bleachers, speedboat, confessional, stand of trees, and Finland.

**RELATED AWARDS:**

The Valorous Conduct Medal for Heavy Petting

The Intrepid Tonsillar Explorer's Badge of Courage and Skill

The Mystery Bruises Medal for Making Out in Tightly Enclosed Spaces

The Order of the Green Knees for Getting Down and Dirty in the Great Outdoors

The Big Ol' Hickey Badge of Excess Enthusiasm

The Judicial Order of Restraint

"Everything's new! Everything's a surprise! And it lasts for hours! Heavy petting is heavy awesome!"
—*Alex Spencer, 16, Tustin, California*

MEDAL REGISTRY No. L-25 | FAMILY: Love | CATEGORY: Singlehood

# The Presidential Medal for Bravery in the Face of Unknown Nudity

**AWARDED FOR:** Entering a state of nudity with a new partner for the first time and surviving the awkwardness and pressure of mutual evaluation.

**MEDAL:** Mirrorlike chrome finish.

**RIBBON:** Ten parallel flesh-colored stripes range from pale to dark, symbolizing the naked rainbow of revealed humankind.

**ON REVERSE:** "It is not the mountain we conquer but ourselves."
—Sir Edmund Hillary

**CLASPS & CLUSTERS:** A Silver Mask Pin is added for adopting a poker face at lightning speed when debut nudity reveals scars in excess of twelve inches or a quantity of nipples greater than two.

**RELATED AWARDS:**

The Order of the Sainted Jordache for Miraculous Asset Management

The Shared Humanity Award for Adjusted Expectations

The Atavistic Tail-Acceptance Medal

The Hidden-Treasure Cross with Jackpot Clusters

"Can I tell you how much I love clothes? They make everybody look taller, thinner, and altogether sexier than they really are. Most of all, me. And suddenly there you are. Naked. No more slimming pinstripes, nothing to lift or separate you. Or them! Just how big is the difference between fantasy and reality? Just how apparent is my reaction? And how am I coming off? Too skinny? Too zaftig? Too pale? Too *some*thing? It's *Matrix*-style bullet time from hell!"
—*George Bertheim, 36, Boston, Massachusetts*

# KISS AND TELL

## THE PROPER ETIQUETTE OF MEDAL DISPLAY

As with courtship, in polite society a number of conventions
have evolved around the sharing of one's love medals.
When a person is lucky enough to earn one or more honors
or commendations for bravery in the search for true love,
these mores should be respected for the benefit of all.

### ON YOUR PERSON

The golden rule of medal display
is "Display medals *for* others, not
*to* others." A medal should be an
invitation to talk about one's experience, not a weapon of vanity. One
must always be considerate of com-
panions, with the knowledge that
medals can speak as loudly as words.

It is considered bad form, for
example, to wear one's True Love
medal when visiting a friend who
has just suffered a terrible heartbreak, or who is currently bemoan-
ing his or her uncoupled status.
One must also refrain from using
medals as passive-aggressive relationship tools. If physical contact
is lacking, to cite one instance, the
corresponding frustration should
be introduced in conversation, not
by wearing one's Six-Month Involuntary Abstinence Cross to dinner.

It is vital to analyze prospective
social settings when assembling

one's rack. Will there be family
present? All medals relating to
physical intimacy should be left at
home so as to avoid any potential
embarrassment.

Particular care must be taken when
wearing one's medals in the presence of an ex-partner. While there
is understandable temptation to use
one's rack to revisit past grievances
or demonstrate recent romantic
accomplishments, one should
behave with grace (if not actual
kindness) and with the knowledge
that there is the potential for
mutual assured destruction in any
public ex-on-ex exchange of medal
information.

As a matter of common courtesy
and self-respect, medals are to
be worn in good condition (a
polished medal is a happy medal)
and hanging straight and true from
a clean, wrinkle-free ribbon.

## IN HOME OR OFFICE

Again, it's critical to contemplate context when thinking about how to display love medals. Certain awards are not fit for the family room or the front office. A private study, however, might be the perfect place to showcase one's entire uncensored medalography. The distinction between "showcase" and "show off" must be drawn here—one's goal is to share, not to boast, and proper placement will help ensure this line is not crossed.

As with good medal hygiene when wearing awards, it's important to demonstrate respect for hard-earned love medals in interior display. A shadowbox, wall-mounted or placed on a desk or credenza, is an ideal way to exhibit one's treasures, simultaneously providing a dignified frame and keeping out dust. A dark velvet lining is recommended to highlight the vivid colors of the ribbons, possibly themed in accordance with the medals themselves (for example, black for breakup, maroon for mid-relationship, etc.). Note that no matter the depth of the frame, whether full shadowbox or merely deep picture, under no circumstances is the face of a medal to be pressed against the glass.

Subtle spotlights will bring out the medals' full luster and demonstrate one's commitment to love. It is best, however, to keep awards away from direct sunlight, as ribbon color will fade, particularly in those issued after 1993, when romantically irrelevant environmental legislation compelled the discontinuance of light-fast ribbon dyes containing cadmium, cobalt, and arsenic, which, while vibrant, proved also to be toxic (it is further advised to avoid direct skin-to-ribbon contact on medals issued before 1994, even in an erotic context).

---

### CARING FOR LOVE MEDALS
As small works of art, medals demand care and maintenance.

- Before display, bearers should apply a small dab of Bilik's Medal Polish (soaps, detergents, or furniture polish must be avoided at all costs, as they may dull, discolor, or corrode the surface of the award, doing lasting damage) and buff both obverse and reverse with a soft, lint-free cloth.

- If medals are displayed in the open, without protection from the environment, they should be dusted with a soft ostrich feather once a week, wiped with a cloth every month, and polished every six months.

- A few strips of adhesive tape will lift most dust and grime from medal ribbons and velvet box-liners. Wrinkled ribbons may be pressed with a low iron between two clean towels. Minor stains can be removed with mild detergent and a toothbrush.

THE MOLTEN MEDAL FOR OVERWHELMING SEX APPEAL

# The Molten Medal for Overwhelming Sex Appeal

**AWARDED FOR:** **Being a person of supreme hot-hot-hotness, a human garden of earthly delights, and an overall dish, who sizzles in such a manner as to leave others helpless with ravenous desire.**

**MEDAL:** Though struck from highly heat-resistant bronze, it frequently melts on its alluring bearer.

**RIBBON:** Scorching hot yellow, orange, and red to symbolize the center of the sun.

**ON REVERSE:** "You're too sexy for this medal."

**RELATED AWARDS:** The Va-Va-Voom Star in Gold with Pinup Clusters

The Burning-Love Medal of Extraordinary Hunkitude

The Shirt-Ripper Star of Uncontrollable Passion

The Squozen Lemon Medal of Excess Juicy Gorgeousness

The "Few, the Proud, the Ludicrously Gorgeous" Citation for Ranking in the 99.999th Percentile of Hubba-Hubba

"How is a bombshell like you not a violation of a nuclear arms treaty or something? It's just not fair! You can't expect any sort of rational conversation from me when you're just so insanely *sexy*!"
—*Devon Gibson, 32, Culver City, California*

"I would like to fry eggs on your hot, rippling abs and have a picnic on your cheekbones. That's all. Yes, I'm objectifying you, and that's just too damn bad. You're simply much too delicious to keep myself in check."
—*Maria Margulies, 27, Minneapolis, Minnesota*

THE FIGHT-OR-FLIGHT COMMENDATION

FOR GROWING INTIMACY

# The Fight-or-Flight Commendation for Growing Intimacy

**AWARDED FOR:** Feeling the beginnings of true intimacy and resisting the urge to create a sudden excuse to terminate the relationship in favor of the known comfort of solitude.

**MEDAL:** Issued in heavyweight, blast furnace–melted cast iron to remind the bearer to stay the course.

**RIBBON:** Solid blue, to soothe the nerves.

**ON REVERSE:** Around the medal's perimeter, "Don't worry—you'll be fine. Don't worry—you'll be fine. Don't worry—you'll be fine."

**RELATED AWARDS:** The "I Don't Think I Can Be with Anybody Who Enjoys/Wears/Eats/Doesn't Read/Listens to _____" Copout Cross

The Deep-Breath Medal of Conscious Panic Abatement

The Reach Out Your Hand and Let Them Pick Up Your Scent Citation for Calming a Skittish Partner

The "Marsha, Marsha, Marsha" Medal of Excess Egocentrism

The Insight Star for Recognizing You're Not the Only One Who's Scared

The "Man Up" Medal of Standing Your Ground Against Your Own Fears

"I like Jim. I think I could love him. So why do I keep thinking of leaving? I *have* always hated those nasty sandals he loves so much. Ugh. And the way he orders the same thing at each restaurant? How much moo goo gai pan can one man eat in a month? But I guess I'll stick it out for now. I can always break it off after the holidays."

—*Kelly Vogler, 35, Council Bluffs, Iowa*

THE EXALTED ORDER OF THE HONEY BEAR FOR SUCCESSFUL PET-NAME EXCHANGE

MUFFIN (1996-2001)

POOKIE (2003)

WILSON (2005-2009)

PUMPKIN (2010-        )

# The Exalted Order of the Honey Bear for Successful Pet-Name Exchange

AWARDED FOR: Exchange of pet names and continuous use of same in situations both private and public (where appropriate) while maintaining an air of residual dignity and good humor.

---

MEDAL: Bronze, with a delightful honey glaze.

RIBBON: Four vertical stripes (left to right): brown (muffin), white (sugar), dark brown (cookie), and pink (sweet cheeks).

ON REVERSE: "Mellita, domi adsum!" (Honey, I'm home!).

CLASPS & CLUSTERS: Dated clasps commemorate the bearer's pet names throughout the course of his or her past relationships, up to the current term(s) of endearment.

---

RELATED AWARDS: The Adam in the Garden of Eden Award for Rapidly Evolving Pet Nomenclature

The Curbed-Enthusiasm Cross for Quitting While You're Ahead

The Dignity Recovery Medal for Issuing a Successful Pet-Name Veto

The Blissful Ignorance Commendation for Failing to Notice the Onset of Nausea in Your Friends

---

"We had been dating for maybe two months when we first gave each other serious pet names. I started out as 'Lumpy' on account of my favorite baggy sweater. That became 'Lump,' then 'Lump-Lump,' then 'Lumpy-Loo,' which is where I drew the line. Now we've settled on 'Lumpy.' My last girlfriend just wouldn't stop calling me 'Pookie.' No one deserves that."

—*Gideon Gottfried, 28, Decatur, Georgia*

Medal Registry No. L-29 | Family: Love | Category: Relationship

# The Public Displays of Affection Citation

**AWARDED FOR:** Freely engaging in such visible demonstrations as holding hands, walking down the street arm in arm, and exchanging kisses.

---

**MEDAL:** Unabashed chrome-plated steel.

**RIBBON:** Two pink ribbons overlapping with no visible light between them.

**ON REVERSE:** "Behold!"

**CLASPS & CLUSTERS:** A Sound Personal Judgment Clasp is awarded on behalf of the citizenry at large for maintaining the delicate balance between romantic enthusiasm and reasonable decorum.

---

**RELATED AWARDS:**

The Golden Liplock Star

The Cheek-to-Cheek Cross with Hand in Your Back Pocket

The Pat-on-the-Butt Commendation for Successfully Executed Pats on the Butt

The Notable Citation for Successfully Ignoring Others' Stares

The "Get a Room" Elicitation Award

The Lingering-Gaze Medal with Rotating Hypnoswirls

---

"Public lewdness … whatever. So we got a little carried away! Even the judge laughed when she saw the surveillance video. They don't call it Miracle Whip for nothing. Best fifty hours of community service ever."
—*Bob Tremaine, 58, Omaha, Nebraska*

"I'll never look at a bus stop the same way again."
—*Mitzi Levinson, 57, Omaha, Nebraska*

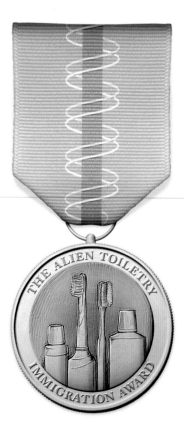

Medal Registry No. L-30 | Family: Love | Category: Relationship

# The Alien Toiletry Immigration Award

**AWARDED FOR:** The peaceful introduction of one person's toiletry items into the other's home bathroom environment.

**MEDAL:** Minted from sterling silver, a compound with actual germ-killing properties, that consists of 925 parts silver and 75 parts copper, symbolizing the small foreign intrusion that increases the hygienic strength of the resulting alloy.

**RIBBON:** Minty fresh, with two thin waxed white lines wound around a fluoridated center stripe of bracing blue to commemorate a new level of togetherness.

**ON REVERSE:** "E pluribus bathroom."

**CLASPS & CLUSTERS:** A silver toothpaste-tube top is awarded for reaching a negotiated settlement of daily operational procedure, including but not limited to overhand versus underhand installation of toilet paper, squeezing of toothpaste from the top or bottom, etc.

**RELATED AWARDS:** The Stranger in a Strange Land Medal for the First Weekend Spent Together

The Legally Binding Side-of-the-Bed Selection Commendation

The "Good Boy" Cross for Pet-Sitting Your Partner's Animal Companion(s)

The "Your Drawer" Annexation Award

The Order of the Genie for Gaining Independent Garage Access

The Golden House Key with Alarm Code Clusters

"To be honest, I just forgot to take my shaving kit one Sunday night, but when Kat told me that it was sweet of me to keep things at her apartment ... who am I to protest?"
—*Dalton Owen, 29, Baltimore, Maryland*

# MEDALS BY NUMBERS
## ILLUSTRIOUS STATISTICS

The issuance of love medals has wielded its own impact on the sociological, psychological, and anthropological landscapes; as they say, opinions are like exes—everybody's got one.

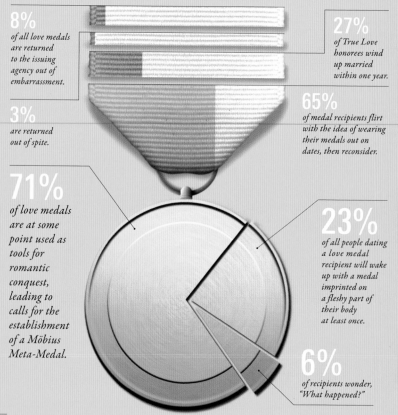

**8%**
*of all love medals are returned to the issuing agency out of embarrassment.*

**27%**
*of True Love honorees wind up married within one year.*

**65%**
*of medal recipients flirt with the idea of wearing their medals out on dates, then reconsider.*

**3%**
*are returned out of spite.*

**71%**
*of love medals are at some point used as tools for romantic conquest, leading to calls for the establishment of a Möbius Meta-Medal.*

**23%**
*of all people dating a love medal recipient will wake up with a medal imprinted on a fleshy part of their body at least once.*

**6%**
*of recipients wonder, "What happened?"*

**51%** of lovers appreciate the awards their current paramours received during previous relationships.

**21%** of friends covet their friends' medals and secretly think they deserve them more.

**34%** of medal recipients think it isn't better to have loved and lost than never to have loved at all.

**12%** of romantic partners wonder why their partners got medals at all.

**37%** of men will receive a love medal during their reproductive years.

**10%** of men would readily trade their medal for a slice of pizza.

**53%** of women will receive a love medal between the ages of 14 and 70, some suspiciously self-awarded.

THE "HELLO, IT'S ME" MEDAL

OF LOWERED MASKS AND BROKEN WALLS

# The "Hello, It's Me" Medal of Lowered Masks and Broken Walls

**AWARDED FOR:** Developing the trust and confidence necessary to let down one's guard and fully reveal oneself.

**MEDAL:** Gold exposed from behind a crumbling wall of iron.

**RIBBON:** Cream ribbon revealed by a diagonally draped flap of red velvet symbolizing a pulled-back curtain.

**ON REVERSE:** "Hi."

**CLASPS & CLUSTERS:** An Opened Vault Door Pin is added for revealing particularly deep and/or dark secrets from one's past, including but not limited to acts of malfeasance, neediness, or modern dance.

**RELATED AWARDS:**

The Secret Playlist Award for Revealing Your Actual Favorite Music

The Low-Mood Admission Cross

The "Thank God—Me Too" Citation for Admitting You're Just a Little More Boring than That

The "Thank God—Me Neither" Citation for Being Able to Skip the Art-House Film in Favor of a Popcorn Movie

The Order of the Blessed Exhalation

The Sexiness Maintenance Medal for Not Taking Personal Comfort Too Far

"It's not like I was hiding who I really was when we started dating, but there was definitely some...judicious editing."
—*Kevin Mendeluk, 27, Port Alice, Canada*

"You can't hold your breath forever. At some point you have to trust that he'll still love you in a baggy T-shirt."
—*Frank Melville, 29, Port Alice, Canada*

The "ORDER OF THE BLESSED PLURAL PRONOUN" AWARD

we

FOR PUBLIC FORMATION OF UNIT

# The "Order of the Blessed Plural Pronoun" Award for Public Formation of Unit

AWARDED FOR: **Making sustained and consistent use of "we" and "us" in social situations, publicly acknowledging the status transition from singles to couple.**

MEDAL: Grade 36 titanium alloy, containing 45 percent niobium, merging two separate metals into a substance considerably stronger than the sum of its parts.

RIBBON: Two separate ribbons, one ebony, the other ivory, are folded in an over-under fashion to create a harmoniously melded spiral.

ON REVERSE: "We hold this us to be self-evident."

CLASPS & CLUSTERS: Silver Venn Diagram Clusters of Bravery are awarded for revealing coupledom if a hostile reaction can be expected, involving such pairings as dog and cat people, Israelis and Palestinians, original and *Next Generation* Trekkies, Lincoln impersonators and Civil War reenactors (Confederates), etc.

RELATED AWARDS:

| | |
|---|---|
| The Rufus Wheeler Peckham Medal of the Super-Secret Recurring In-Joke | The Nervous-Laugh Star for Being Publicly Mistaken for a Married Couple |
| The Postmaster General's Cross for the First Cosigned Postcard | The Virginia Woof Medal for Adopting and Naming a Pet Together |
| The Joyful-But-Still-Awkward-Moment Medal for Telling Your Parents | The "Hi, Honey, I'm Home!" Joint-Lease Medal |

"We really wish we could stay, but we have a two-for-one pass for the new *Romeo and Juliet* production in Weehawken."
—*Ethan Phillips, 33, and Nicole Johnson, 33, Secaucus, New Jersey*

THE PARENTAL INSPECTION MEDAL

MR. & MRS. MORITA

LENNY & JUDY

MARGOT & LT. COL. JARVIS

# The Parental Inspection Medal

AWARDED FOR: **Completing the initial meeting of one's partner's parents and laying the foundation for eventual family acceptance.**

MEDAL: Bronze, with brutally sharpened edges.

RIBBON: Olive, brown, and black camouflage pattern, representing the desire to blend in with one's surroundings without startling potentially aggressive wildlife.

ON REVERSE: "It's so nice to finally meet you!"

CLASPS & CLUSTERS: Brass clasps are issued with the names of parents the bearer has met, using the names they requested be used in addressing them.

RELATED AWARDS:

The Multiple Family Holiday Navigation Cross

The Exemplary Conduct Star for Charming the Quasi-In-Laws

The Esprit de Corps Commendation for Standing by Your Partner in the Face of Familial Pressure

The Weird-Cousin Deflection Medal

The "Hiya, Stretch!" Medal for Receiving a Family Nickname

The "Bombs Are Thicker than Water" Cross for Bonding With Your Partner's Father Over the History Channel

The Parsley, Sage, Rosemary, and Thyme Medal for Complimenting Mom's Secret Recipe

"I knew they'd love me. I mean, how could they not, especially when they were going to see how happy I made their son? I just wish he would have warned me not to call Dr. Fortwängler 'dad' right away."

—*Carol Higginbotham, 38, Shaker Heights, Ohio*

MEDAL REGISTRY No. L-34 | FAMILY: Love | CATEGORY: Relationship

# The Relationship War Zone Medal for Courage Under Irrational Fire

**AWARDED FOR:** Withstanding a sudden onslaught of aggression from one's partner while laboring under the mistaken assumption that things are going well.

**MEDAL:** Issued in shattered and charred steel.

**RIBBON:** A white ribbon of surrender, shot through by small-arms fire.

**ON REVERSE:** "Ceterum censeo [Nickelback] esse delendam" (furthermore, I am of the opinion that Nickelback must be destroyed). —Cato the Elder

**RELATED AWARDS:**

The Sarcastic-Comeback-Suppression Medal of Peace

The Road-to-Hell Star for Seeing Your Good Intentions Backfire

The "You're Gonna Wear *That* Tonight?" Medal of the Exploratory Border Incursion

The Declaration of All-Out War for Bringing My Mother Into This

The Order of the Bell that Can't Be Unrung for Saying Something You Never Ever Should've Said

The Scorched-Earth Citation for Hurtful Generalization

The "How Dare You?" Cross for Hinting at a Monthly Biological Event

"Why would anybody start a massive fight over cat litter? Cat litter? Really? I just try to lay low and let it pass."
—*Julie Lastrow, 52, Austin, Texas*

"Oh great! Yes—lay low! Because I'm just being irrational, right? God forbid you should actually listen to what I'm telling you. Screw you and the horse you rode in on!"
—*Jamie Fisk, 54, Austin, Texas*

Medal Registry No. L-35 | Family: Love | Category: Relationship

# The Unit Commendation for Mutual Forgiveness

**AWARDED FOR:** Sincerely acknowledging that things said in the heat of an argument were hurtful, unproductive, and, for the most part, demonstrably false; making a sincere effort to address valid points in order to forge a lasting peace; and moving forward without holding a grudge.

**MEDAL:** Heat-tempered steel that is visibly scuffed.

**RIBBON:** Light gray, symbolizing the lifting clouds of gun smoke, with a center stripe of hopeful bright green.

**ON REVERSE:** "I'm sorry." "Me too."

**CLASPS & CLUSTERS:** An Olive Branch Clasp, AKA the Kick 'Em When They're Down Pin, is affixed to the ribbon to demonstrate forgiveness of particularly grievous attacks on known areas of insecurity.

**RELATED AWARDS:** The Nobel Peace Prize

The Hint-of-a-Smile Star for Connecting Across the Divide

The Order of Saved Face

The "I Want To Re-Hold Your Hand" Medal of Timid Physical Rapprochement

The "Let's Never Fight Again" Cross with Makeup-Sex Clusters

"I don't know what happened. All this fury came out of nowhere when he finished the last of the wine. I wouldn't blame him if he never wanted to see me again after what I said, but he wasn't such an angel, either. Thank goodness he's willing to move on, and so am I. I think the sex helped."
—*Jan Coleridge, 68, Sioux Falls, South Dakota*

# THE OPPOSITE OF GLORY
## DATING DEMERITS AND REPRIMANDS

One strives to accentuate the positive and reward the meritorious, but where there is light there is also shadow: not all men are princes, all women angels. Fortunately there exist scarlet letters of love to warn the innocent. Caveat amator!

BEWARE!

```
DEMERITS FOR INSUFFICIENT EFFORT
AND ERODED STANDARDS OF CONDUCT
==================================

The Partial Misogyny-Suppression Cross

The Exemplary Conduct Citation for Talking
Without Your Mouth Full

The Golden Shop-Vac Thoughtful Gift Commendation

The Dutch Foreign Legion for Almost Always Paying Your Half

The Exemplary Service Medal for Sexy Underwear
on Your Birthday and Maybe Christmas

The Implied Compliment Cross

The Intermittent Excellence in Personal Hygiene Star

The 10-Percent-by-Volume Medal for Occasionally
Allowing Your Date to Join the Conversation

The Barely Condescending Medal

The Indomitable Spirit Star for Attempting
a Booty Call After Not Calling for Months


REPRIMANDS AND CALLOUS MISDEMEANORS
===================================

The Damage-Control Medal for a Swift Apology
After a Forgotten First Date

The Advanced Reticence Cross for Never Calling
```

CONSOLATION MEDALS FOR THE IRREDEEMABLY WIMPY
====================================================

The Adorably Clueless Cross for Being Blatantly Betrayed

The Low-Self-Esteem Star for Assuming the Blame Regardless of Circumstance

The Grand Gesture Medal of Attempted Reconciliation by Means of Personal Debasement

The Unexpected Loneliness Cross with Grief Clasp

The Utter Defeat Citation

The Cover-of-Darkness Citation for Never Staying the Night

The Order of Casual Disregard

The Flip-Flops and Heels Medal for Careless Wardrobe Mismatch

The Order-of-the-Oops Medal for Forgetting an Airport Pickup

The Google Know-It-All Cross with iPhone Clusters

The Searing-Honesty Star for Hyperaccurate Personal Critiques


PERMANENT-RECORD ENTRIES OF DATING FELONY
====================================================

The Willful Omission Medal for Hiding the Fact that You Have Kids

The "Liar Liar Pants on Fire" Brand for Pretending You're
Something that You're Most Certainly Not

The Barnacle Cross for Dating Solely to Gain Room and Board

The Outgoing Personality Citation for Blatant Flirtation

The Obvious Obfuscation and Evasion Cross for Suspicious Conduct

The Relationship Jujitsu Medal with Brass Balls

The Mirror-Universe Medal with Reality Distortion Field

The Houdini Medal of Misdirection and Sudden Disappearance

The Drama Desk Award for Most Tempestuous Walkout

Medal Registry No. L-36 | Family: Love | Category: Relationship

# The Open Bathroom Door Negotiation Medal

**AWARDED FOR:** **Reaching a level of mutual comfort that allows for an honest negotiation of boundaries relating to moments of mundane personal hygiene.**

**MEDAL:** A considerate alloy of nickel and aluminum.

**RIBBON:** Open and unabashed yellow with a wide black vertical center stripe to block out anything that need not be seen.

**ON REVERSE:** "Life is a tragedy when seen in close-up, but a comedy in long-shot." —Charlie Chaplin

**CLASPS & CLUSTERS:** A Silver Toilet Roll Cluster is awarded in recognition of any retinal, olfactory, or spiritual damage suffered before negotiations could take place.

**RELATED AWARDS:** The Intestinal Pressure Control Commendation

The Blessed Veil of Courtesy Star for Concealed Grooming Activity

The Separate Laundry Cross

The Order of the Shared Suitcase

The Expanded Comfort Zone Medal

The Audible-Emission Forgiveness Citation

"I love living with Karen, but watching her go to the bathroom? Not the kind of intimacy I'm looking for. Thank you, though."
—*Richard Mohenjo-Daro, 41, Astoria, Oregon*

"From the horrified squeal, you'd have thought I was chewing off my toenails with my bare teeth. If I were Sandy, I'd be happy that my boyfriend was still limber enough to get his foot in the sink and reach it with the clippers.
—*Clarence Watkins, 56, Crown Heights, New York*

# The Strong-Shoulder Medal of Support in the Face of Personal Tragedy

AWARDED FOR: Offering solace and support, both material and spiritual, in one's partner's moment of personal tragedy, revealing a heretofore unexpected reserve of compassion, emotional generosity, and overall kindness of spirit.

MEDAL: Always-dependable stainless steel, covered with warm copper plating.

RIBBON: Comforting tan-and-black-plaid flannel.

ON REVERSE: "I'm here when you need me."

CLASPS & CLUSTERS: A Wadded Kleenex Kluster is added for providing steadfast support in situations of complete emotional collapse, regardless of potential mucus danger posed to garments or furniture.

RELATED AWARDS:
The Shared Pain Cross

The Heart-of-Gold Medal for Offering Crucial Administrative Assistance in a Time of Grief

The Order of the Open Ear

The Commendation for Voluntary Domestic Servitude in Times of Professional Overload

The "Did You Hear About This One?" Medal of Gentle Humor and Topical Distraction

"We'd only been dating for three months when I got the first of all ten graduate school rejections. He never made me feel like an idiot, and he helped me see that starting my own business was better than any PhD. Not only am I an award-winning apiculturist now, but he gets free honey for life!"
—*Jennifer Stinson, 28, Sacramento, California*

THE CASUAL GESTURE OF TRUE KINDNESS

REMOVAL-OF-ALL-DOUBT STAR

# The Casual Gesture of True Kindness Removal-of-All-Doubt Star

**AWARDED FOR:** Revealing one's true core of generosity in a selfless, spontaneous, offhand way during an otherwise unremarkable everyday moment without expecting special acknowledgment or gratitude.

**MEDAL:** Matte tin plating over a true gold core, visible through the exposed golden petal at the heart of the rose.

**RIBBON:** Warm red with three vertical gold stripes.

**ON REVERSE:** "It is difficult to know at what moment love begins; it is less difficult to know that it has begun."
—Henry Wadsworth Longfellow

**CLASPS & CLUSTERS:** A Golden Index Card Clasp is added to the ribbon for seemingly superhuman feats of memory regarding one's partner's personal tastes and preferences months or years after a casual mention.

**RELATED AWARDS:** The Order of the Esoteric Sausage for Procuring a Rare Childhood Treat by Means of International Reconnaissance and Shipping

The Well-Timed Tourism Medal for Knowing When to Book a Romantic Getaway

The Advanced Antiquing Cross

The Grand-Gesture Cross with Two-Carat Diamond Ring

The Sweetness Cross for Surrendering the Last Bite of Dessert

"I'm a grown man, but every now and again Sam will make me a PB&J and slip it into my briefcase with a little note. Makes me grin like a fool when I find it."
—*Tyler Harrison, 42, Calabasas, California*

Medal Registry No. L-40 | Family: Love | Category: True Love

# The One-in-a-Million Medal of True Love Recognition and Reciprocation

**AWARDED FOR:** Finding and appreciating one's true love, investing the courage and effort necessary to open oneself to him or her, accepting him or her as a real human being, and being accepted in return.

**MEDAL:** Solid gold polished to a high shine.

**RIBBON:** Sky blue with radiating beams of gold united by a thin line of lovely red.

**ON REVERSE:** "'Tis brave to search for love but braver still to let love find you."

**CLASPS & CLUSTERS:** A gold star for extraordinary bravery and tenacity is affixed if true love was achieved in the wake of three or more consecutive failed relationships or directly following five or more years spent alone.

**RELATED AWARDS:**

The Blissful Glow and Dreamy Smile Dead-Giveaway Commendation

The Newman-Woodward Medal of Showing 'Em How It's Done

The Etta James Medal of Classy Relief

The "What's Next?" Star for Riding Toward a New Horizon

The Enlightened Humility Star for Never Turning Your Good Fortune into Pat Advice for Your Single Friends

The "To Be Continued" Cross of Future Adventures

"Thank God I found you!"
—*Sam Lowell, 42, New York, New York*

"What took you so long?"
—*Anna Simmons, 39, Los Angeles, California*

2012 — The Golden Pyramid Star for Surviving the End of the Mayan Calendar

2027 — The Turing Medal for Entering a Serious Relationship with an Artificial Intelligence

2034 — The Grand Spandex Star with Lipo Clusters for Looking Great in Your Skintight Cybersuit

2059 — The Petaflop Medal for Generating a Trillion Compliments per Second

2072 — The Tiny Bubbles Medal for the First Exchange of Personalized Nanospores

2087 — The "Good Dogbot" Citation for Taking Care of Your Partner's Laserpuppy

2201 — The Glow-of-Love Medal for Traversing the Radioactive Wasteland and Fighting Off Marauding Mutants to Meet Your Partner

2269 — The "Love Conquers All, Even Post-Apocalyptic Zombies" Cross for Romance Under Difficult Circumstances

2270 — The Distributed Computing Star for Dating a Solely Virtual Person

# DATING MEDALS OF TOMORROW

## THE FUTURE OF MEDALS—TODAY!

Technology is moving at an ever-quickening pace, accelerating too fast for our minds, mores, and, yes, hearts to keep up. The only certainty is that humanity will somehow adapt its primordial need for love to the realities of a rocket-powered future.

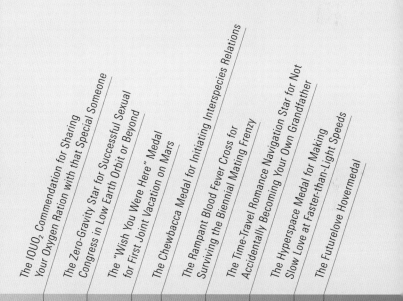

The IOUO₂ Commendation for Sharing Your Oxygen Ration with that Special Someone — 2315

The Zero-Gravity Star for Successful Sexual Congress in Low Earth Orbit or Beyond — 2345

The "Wish You Were Here" Medal for First Joint Vacation on Mars — 2398

The Chewbacca Medal — 3763

The Rampant Blood Fever Cross for Initiating Interspecies Relations Surviving the Biennial Mating Frenzy — 4018

The Time-Travel Romance Navigation Star for Not Accidentally Becoming Your Own Grandfather — 1977, 4023

The Hyperspace Medal for Making Slow Love at Faster-than-Light Speeds — 12081

The Futurelove Hovermedal — 22179

# LET'S GO OVER THIS AGAIN
## THE ILLUSTRATED MEDAL INDEX

**14** The Shadow-of-a-Doubt Medal of Creeping Disenchantment

**16** The Order of the Ostrich

**18** The Advanced Pragmatism Cross

**20** The Pandering Star

**22** The Six-Month Involuntary Abstinence Cross

**26** The Worst-of-Times Medal for Breakup Survival

**28** The Exceptional Courage Badge for Enduring the First Day After

**30** The Separation of Collections Commendation

**32** The Sanity Award for Escaping the Breakup-Makeup Cycle

**34** The Long Hard Stare Medal of Personal Failure in Love

**38** The Order of the Golden Pint for Bravery in the Face of Sorrow

**40** The Mutual Friends Diplomacy Award

**42** The Post-Relationship Hibernation Cross

**44** The Self-Respect Recovery Star

**46** The Learned Optimism Star

**50** The Silver Lining Cross for a Successful Rebound Fling

**52** The Persistent Online Dating Campaign Medal

**54** The High-Wire Award for Forging a Friends-with-Benefits Arrangement

**56** The Butterfly Order of the Unexpected Crush

**58** The Gallantry Cross

| | | |
|---|---|---|
| BREAKUP | | 12 |
| SINGLEHOOD | | 14 |
| RELATIONSHIP | | 13 |
| TRUE LOVE | | 1 |

**62**
The First-Kiss Star

**64**
The Legion of Saintly Patience for Waiting by the Phone

**66**
The Unlimited Texting Cross for Stellar Love Notes in 160 Characters or Less

**68**
The Medal of Making Out

**70**
The Presidential Medal for Bravery in the Face of Unknown Nudity

**74**
The Molten Medal for Overwhelming Sex Appeal

**76**
The Fight-or-Flight Commendation for Growing Intimacy

**78**
The Exalted Order of the Honey Bear for Successful Pet-Name Exchange

**80**
The Public Displays of Affection Citation

**82**
The Alien Toiletry Immigration Award

**86**
The "Hello, It's Me" Medal of Lowered Masks and Broken Walls

**88**
The "Order of the Blessed Plural Pronoun" Award for Public Formation of Unit

**90**
The Parental Inspection Medal

**92**
The Relationship War-Zone Medal for Courage Under Irrational Fire

**94**
The Unit Commendation for Mutual Forgiveness

**98**
The Open Bathroom Door Negotiation Medal

**100**
The Order of Saintly Patience in Waiting for the Commitment-Phobic

**102**
The Strong-Shoulder Medal of Support in the Face of Personal Tragedy

**104**
The Casual Gesture of True Kindness Removal-of-All-Doubt Star

**106**
The One-in-a-Million Medal of True Love Recognition and Reciprocation

## It is my strong personal opinion and belief that

_____

*Name of Potential Honoree*

## deserves a Medal of Love.

Over the course of the past _____  ❑ days   ❑ weeks
                                            ❑ months ❑ years
*Length of Service*

❑ *he*  ❑ *she* has demonstrated  ❑ *enduring*  ❑ *extraordinary*  ❑ *heroic*

❑ *persistent*  ❑ *romantic*  ❑ *steadfast*  ❑ *valiant*  ❑ _____

❑ *bravery*  ❑ *care*  ❑ *chivalry*  ❑ *compassion*  ❑ *enthusiasm*

❑ *excellence*  ❑ *endurance*  ❑ *flexibility*  ❑ *good humor*  ❑ *passion*

❑ *patience*  ❑ *resilience*  ❑ *self-control*  ❑ _____

in the pursuit of love, making  ❑ *him*  ❑ *her* worthy
of official recognition. I cite the following example(s)
as proof of  ❑ *his*  ❑ *her* eligibility:

_____

_____

_____

_____

*I certify that the foregoing is true and correct to the best of my knowledge,*
*and I hereby petition that the appropriate Medal of Love be awarded forthwith.*

_____     _____

*Signature*                                              *Date*

_____     _____

*Printed Name*                                         *Email*

Please mail completed form to the Council of Romantic Decorations, c/o Knock Knock,
1635-B Electric Avenue, Venice, CA 90291—or, if you'd rather not deface this book,
you may fill out the electronic form at www.you-deserve-a-medal.com.